BLOGILATES

Sculpt

a protein cookbook

Recipes to feed the joy in fitness.

by Cassey Ho

a note from
Cassey

Food is fuel, but also, it's cultural, it's social, it's emotional, it's identity, it's nostalgia, it's comfort, it's passion, it's celebration! I get so fanatical when I talk about food because when my taste buds light up, my whole world lights up.

When I first started Blogilates back in 2009, my focus was to simply share some fun home workouts. I never actually intended for it to be more than that until my students started asking to see how I lived my life outside of the studio — specifically...how I ate!

Well, good thing — because I LOVE eating and I LOVE food. From posting recipes on my blog to sharing cooking videos on YouTube, I find so much joy playing around in the kitchen, testing ingredients, and experimenting with unusual combinations to create the healthiest (and tastiest) foods to nourish my body, and yours.

I am so excited to share this cookbook with you because each recipe was carefully crafted to make your taste buds swoon. I also wanted to find a very special way to share the launch of my first ever, Sculpt + Debloat Protein Powder with Probiotics! Ahh! I can't believe it's finally happening!

Backstory time.

Nobody knows this, but I actually started developing a protein powder about eight years ago. I was completely obsessed with trying to make the most unique, best tasting, smoothest, easiest-to-cook, plant-based, macronutrient rich formula on the market. I worked with food scientists, recipe developers, a doctor, and multiple labs to try to get my formula just right. But nothing ever quite got there. When I changed one thing, it broke something else. They told me what I wanted was impossible. Iteration after iteration, what I needed you to experience and what was actually happening in the lab were just not aligning. After many failed attempts, I was tired. My body was telling me that it was time to end the project.

So...I did.

But you know, true passion never really dies. The fire is always burning inside...just waiting for the right time to ignite...

Well, a couple years ago, I felt something. Something telling me to try again. It was a strong feeling I couldn't ignore.

This time, things were different.

And this time, things worked out.

Sculpt + Debloat is my dream protein powder, finally come to life! I'm obsessed with the way it tastes, the way it cooks, the way it bakes, and what it's been doing for my body on my 90 Day Journey. It's fueling my muscles and also feeding my joy in fitness. Plus...those probiotics are fabulous for keeping my bloat in check.

In this cookbook you'll find an array of options, whether you're vegan, low carb, or have allergies. The recipes are designed to have easy swaps so that no matter which style of eating you follow, you can enjoy these fun, simple, and high-protein foods that will leave you feeling satisfied, but more importantly, fueled up for workouts, and for life in general!

Cassey

@blogilates

PS: Ugh, I so want to invite you over to my house, seat you at my kitchen table, and make some fresh hot protein pancakes for you, drizzled with drippy peanut butter and slathered with syrupy goodness! I know it's a far drive (or plane ride), so instead...promise me that when you take your first bite, to please close your eyes, take a moment to let every taste bud savor the magic, and then clap uncontrollably with pure giddiness, k?! Cuz that's what I'll be doing too!

Contents

Quick Snacks - 95

Desserts - 119

a note about
Ingredients

Protein Powder

When cooking and baking with protein powder, it's helpful to know that they don't all perform the same in recipes. So if you've ever had a recipe flop because you substituted a vegan protein powder, for, say, a whey powder, know that it's not your fault! The composition, volume, ingredients, sweeteners, fillers, and thickeners vary in each brand. Every recipe in this cookbook was designed and tested multiple times using our specific Blogilates Sculpt + Debloat Protein Powder with Probiotics and Blogilates Beauty Collagen Peptides. Our clean ingredients, fiber and choice of natural sweeteners come together in such a way that they not only produce delicious shakes, but create next-level baked good and treats. Should you substitute another brand of powder, your results and bake times may vary greatly.

Sweeteners

Monk fruit sugar is my favorite go-to sweetener. The white and golden versions from Lakanto taste amazing, are low glycemic, and work 1:1 for sugar. You can purchase powdered monk fruit sweetener or buy granular monk fruit and process it in a blender yourself. Feel free to use honey, coconut sugar, date syrup, or your sweetener of choice, knowing that substitutions affect the macros. For our purposes, we wanted to minimize extra carbs by choosing monk fruit to fuel your fitness performance goals, and minimize inflammation. If substituting with pure stevia, know that you'll need far less than each recipe calls for. If substituting a liquid sweetener, such as honey, you'll generally have to adjust the dry ingredients slightly. Straight erythritol, or another brand of monk fruit + erythritol sweetener will likely substitute just fine in each recipe.

Milks

We like the following non-dairy milks: almond, coconut, cashew and macadamia; or a blend, like coconut almond.

Flours

To stay gluten-free we use almond, oat, tapioca, and coconut flours. These cannot always be subbed 1:1, so adjust liquids or amounts as needed. For example, coconut flour absorbs liquids, so to adjust, you need more liquid or less flour. Oat flour is pretty dense, while almond flour is quite light. All substitutions will affect the macros in each recipe. When we use tapioca flour, please note that this is a key ingredient that's hard to substitute.

Chocolate

We use Lily's sugar-free chocolate in our recipes, which can be found online and in many grocery stores. Whole Foods has their own version of a sugar-free semi-sweet chocolate chip, which is a great product as well.

Allergies

If you have a nut allergy, please substitute sunflower butter when nut butter is called for. You can choose your favorite nut-free flour for almond flour, but depending on what you choose, you will have to adjust the ratios slightly. Part of our mission in this cookbook was to develop recipes with nut and nut-free options so that everyone can safely find several that work for their dietary needs.

Protein 101

Protein is one of three macronutrients — nutrients that your body uses in the largest amounts for energy, function, and structure. Carbohydrates and fat are the other two.

When you think of protein, you probably think muscle. And you're right! Protein is key for muscle building, but that's not all we need it for. It also helps with athletic performance, weight loss, and recovery from surgery or illness. You'll find protein pretty much everywhere in the body, including your hair, skin, nails, bones, organs, and tissues.

When you eat protein, it's broken down into amino acids (there are twenty!) that serve a specific purpose in the body. Many are important for structure, while others do cool things like create enzymes and hormones, or carry oxygen in the blood.

How much protein do you need?

Okay, get your pen and paper ready. There's no single protein calculation that will work for everyone. Like everything with nutrition, you have to consider your needs and goals.

For the average, healthy adult who is just looking to maintain a healthy diet, the recommended daily amount (RDA) is 0.8 grams (g) of protein per kilogram (kg) of bodyweight.

If your eyes just glazed over, don't worry! To figure out your weight in kilograms, just divide your weight in pounds by 2.2.

> For example: 150 lb / 2.2 = 68.2 kg
> To figure out protein needs: 0.8 grams x 68.2 kg = 55 g of protein per day

Again, this is just the bare minimum recommendation for people looking to give the body what it needs for general health. Certain health conditions and stressors on the body (injuries, illness, etc.) increase protein needs.

Likewise, your protein needs increase if you're highly active or trying to build muscle.

If you're active — The American College of Sports Medicine recommends 1.2 — 2 grams of protein per kilogram of bodyweight.

If you're building muscle — The recommendation increases to 1.6 — 2.2 grams of protein per kilogram of bodyweight.

Another common recommendation is to aim your protein intake for somewhere between 10-35% of the calories you eat every day. If you're highly active and/or trying to build muscle, aim for the higher end of this range.

Who Should Take a Protein Supplement?

Of course it's possible to meet any protein goal with food. However, people often struggle to meet these goals for many reasons. Maybe planning and preparing meals is too daunting or time-consuming. Maybe your dietary preferences make it difficult to get a variety of high-quality proteins.

Whatever your struggle may be, protein powder is a tool that helps you hit your protein goals consistently. And with everything in fitness, consistency is key. Protein powder is also super convenient for post-workout recovery. Plus, you can use it to make sure you always have healthy, high-protein snacks on hand (that's where this book comes in!) This is so helpful if you struggle to hit your macros or find yourself hungry between meals.

Types of Protein Powder (and How to Know What Is Best for You)

Choosing a protein powder can be...overwhelming. So let's talk about the most common types and how they're different.

Animal-based protein powders:

Whey — Likely the most common type of protein powder you'll see. Whey is made from dairy and is high in branched-chain amino acids (BCAAs), which are great for muscle growth. Whey protein is absorbed quickly, which makes it great for post-workout recovery.

Whey concentrate contains lactose, making it difficult for some people to digest. Whey isolate contains very little lactose.

Casein- Also derived from dairy, casein is digested much more slowly than whey. It gives the body a slow, steady dose of amino acids. This helps with satiety (feeling full) and muscle growth.

Egg — Typically made with egg whites, egg protein is an excellent source of essential amino acids and a great alternative for those with trouble digesting whey or casein.

Plant-based protein powders:

Pea protein — Made from yellow split peas, this is an amazing source of BCAAs. It is absorbed more slowly than whey, but not as slowly as casein. Therefore, pea protein is great for post-workout recovery, muscle growth, and satiety.

Brown rice protein — Another option with a great amino acid profile that is also easy to digest and hypo-allergenic. Brown rice protein is absorbed more slowly than pea protein.

Hemp protein — Hemp protein is unique because it also contains omega-3 fatty acids. Most people find it easy to absorb. However, it's slightly lower in certain amino acids.

Are plant-based protein powders as effective as animal-based proteins like whey?

Absolutely! Several studies show that using plant-based protein powder usually gives similar results as whey protein. Here's the difference between the two types.

We mentioned that protein breaks down into amino acids. Out of the twenty, there are nine that your body cannot make itself. The only way to get them is through food! We call these "essential" amino acids.

Now let's tie this back into protein powders. Animal proteins like whey, casein, and egg protein have all nine essential amino acids, deeming them "complete" proteins. On the other hand, plant-based proteins typically lack at least one of the essential amino acids.

Does that mean plant-based protein powders aren't effective? Nope! All protein sources have different amino acid profiles. That means as long as you're getting some variety in your diet, you're mostly likely getting the "missing" amino acid elsewhere.

We used a blend of yellow pea and organic whole grain brown rice protein in the Blogilates Sculpt and Debloat Protein Powders to create a high-quality, complete source of plant-based protein.

Cooking with Protein

Is it really okay to cook with protein? Maybe you read an article or heard from someone at the gym that cooking "denatures" protein, rendering it useless. Here's the truth.

Denaturing happens, but it's not a bad thing. It just means that the protein becomes "unfolded." This structure change does slightly impact the way it works in the body, but it doesn't destroy the protein or lessen the benefits it gives you.

What is collagen?

Collagen is a type of structural protein found in the skin, connective tissue, muscle, and bones. As we age, collagen production in the body slows down. Environmental factors like UV exposure, smoking, drinking alcohol, and eating a lot of added sugar can also decrease collagen production. This results in wrinkles and other classic signs of aging.

Taking a collagen supplement can support skin health, improving elasticity and hydration. It may also help with joint pain and maintain bone health. Of course since collagen is a protein, it also contributes to muscle growth. Finally, collagen may help your hair and nails grow stronger.

How much do you need? The most common recommendation for generally healthy people is between 2.5 to 15 grams of collagen per day, in terms of safety and effectiveness. Each one-scoop serving of Blogilates Beauty Collagen Peptides provides 10 grams of collagen.

Cooking with collagen — We love how easy it is to cook with collagen! It easily mixes into warm or cold food or beverage recipes and the flavor is totally undetectable.

Bever -ages

Maple Milk Tea Boba

Matcha Bubble Milk Tea

Blackberry Milk Tea

Matcha Latte

Hot Cocoa

Spoonable Chunky Monkey Shake

Chai Smoothie

Almond Blueberry Shake

Birthday Cake Shake

Chocolate Peanut Butter Shake

Peaches & Sweet Cream Shake

Pumpkin Pie Smoothie

Piña Colada Shake

Mint Chip Shake

Chocolate Mocha Shake

Chocolate Covered Raspberry

Maple Milk Tea Boba

"I. Love. Boba! But I wanted to create a version that was dairy-free and low sugar, so I came up with this one and included collagen for extra protein...and all the beauty benefits!"

Yield: 1 serving
Serving Size: 1 beverage
Prep Time: 5 min
Cook Time: 15 min

Ingredients

- ¼ cup tapioca pearls*
- 2 tablespoons maple monk fruit syrup
- 2 black tea bags
- 1 scoop Blogilates Beauty Collagen Peptides
- ½ cup non-dairy milk
- 2-3 tablespoons powdered monk fruit sweetener, divided
- ½ teaspoon vanilla extract

Method

1. Bring a pot of water to a boil and add tapioca pearls. Once pearls have floated to the top (about 3 minutes), cover pot and boil for 3-5 minutes, until soft and chewy. *Note: instructions may vary depending on the type of tapioca pearls. Follow instructions on the package for best results.

2. Drain, then place in a small saucepan with the syrup over low heat for 2 minutes. Remove from heat to cool and absorb the maple flavor (if you like it sweeter, use 3 tablespoons).

3. Make the tea by boiling ½ cup of water and steeping the tea bags for 5 minutes. Remove tea bags, add 1 tablespoon of powdered sweetener, and allow tea to cool.

4. Add the collagen, milk, remaining 1-2 tablespoons of sweetener and vanilla to a large measuring cup, and use a frother to aerate the mixture. (If you don't have a frother, blend in a mini blender for 20 seconds).

5. To assemble, pour the tapioca pearls and syrup to the bottom of a large glass. Fill the glass halfway with ice. Pour the tea over the ice, followed by the milk mixture. Stir slightly with a boba straw, and enjoy.

Note: Tapioca pearls are available from specific grocery stores and on Amazon.

Calories: 163 | Protein: 10g | Fat: 1g | Carbs: 52g | Fiber: 8g | Net-Carbs: 20g

Matcha
Bubble
Milk Tea

"I love matcha. I love boba. And I love me a healthy version of everything. This tastes like the one from the tea shop! I swear!"

Yield: 1 serving
Serving Size: 1 beverage
Prep Time: 5 min
Cook Time: 15 min

Ingredients

- ¼ cup tapioca pearls*
- 1 tablespoon honey
- 1-1½ teaspoons matcha green tea powder**
- ½ cup hot water
- ½ cup non-dairy milk
- 1 scoop Blogilates Beauty Collagen Peptides
- 1½ tablespoons powdered monk fruit
      sweetener, divided
- ½ teaspoon vanilla extract

Method

1. Bring a pot of water to a boil and add tapioca pearls. Once the pearls have floated to the top (about 3 minutes), cover the pot and boil for 3-5 minutes, until soft and chewy.

*Note: instructions may vary depending on the type of tapioca pearls. Follow instructions on the package for best results.

2. Drain, then place in a small saucepan with the honey, stirring over low heat for 3 minutes. Remove from heat to cool.

3. *Whisk together the amount of matcha you like with 1/2 cup of hot water and 1 tablespoon powdered sweetener, then set aside to cool.

4. Froth or blend the milk, collagen, remaining powdered sweetener and vanilla until frothy.

5. Assemble the beverage by adding the honey tapioca to the bottom of a large glass or pint mason jar. Fill the glass halfway with ice. Pour the matcha on top, followed by the milk. Serve immediately with a boba straw.

Calories: 230 | Protein: 11g | Fat: 3g | Carbs: 59g | Fiber: 2g | Net-Carbs: 39g

Blackberry
Milk Tea

"I mean, how is that not THE prettiest drink you've ever seen in your life??"

Yield: 1 serving
Serving Size: 1 beverage
Prep Time: 5 min
Cook Time: 3 min
Chill Time: 15 min

Ingredients

- 1 Blackberry or blueberry tea bag
- ½ cup boiling water
- 3 tablespoons powdered monk fruit
      sweetener, divided
- 6 blackberries
- ½ cup non-dairy milk
- 1 scoop Blogilates Beauty Collagen Peptides
- 1 teaspoon vanilla extract
- ½ cup ice

Method

1. Steep the tea in 1/2 cup boiling water according to brand instructions. Cool in the fridge for 15 minutes. Remove tea bag. Add 1 tablespoon of the powdered sweetener.

2. Add blackberries and 1 tablespoon of the powdered sweetener to a tall glass, smash the berries, and stir to incorporate the sweetener. It should end up looking a bit like chunky jam.

3. Using a milk frother, combine the milk, collagen, vanilla, and remaining tablespoon of sweetener.

4. When ready to assemble, add ice to the berries. Pour the tea over the ice, followed by the frothed milk. Insert a large staw stir lightly and enjoy!

Calories: 79 | Protein: 10g | Fat: 1g | Carbs: 41g | Fiber: 2g | Net-Carbs: 3g

Matcha Latte

"It's like a hug in a cup. So warm, it fills my soul with pure joy."

Yield: 1 serving
Serving Size: 1 beverage
Prep Time: 3 min
Cook Time: 3 min

Ingredients

- ½ cup non-dairy milk
- ½ cup water
- 1 scoop Blogilates Beauty Collagen Peptides
- 1 tablespoon powdered monk fruit sweetener
- 1 teaspoon matcha green tea powder
- ½ teaspoon vanilla extract
- ¼ teaspoon cinnamon

Method

1. Heat the milk and water in a small saucepan or in the microwave. Be careful not to boil it, as this can change the taste of the matcha.

2. Add to a mini blender with the remaining ingredients and process until combined and slightly foamy (you can also just use a milk frother). Pour into a large mug, and enjoy immediately.

Calories: 74 | Protein: 11g | Fat: 1g | Carbs: 16g | Fiber: 1g | Net-Carbs: 3g

Hot Cocoa

"You get the beauty benefits of collagen and the rich creaminess of chocolate in under 5 minutes with this satisfying cup of cocoa. My version helps keep you full, unlike regular cocoa which is pretty much straight sugar."

Yield: 1 serving
Serving Size: 1 beverage
Prep Time: 3 min
Cook Time: 3 min

Ingredients

- ¾ cup non-dairy milk
- ½ cup water
- 1 scoop Blogilates Beauty Collagen Peptides
- 2 tablespoons powdered monk fruit sweetener (or to taste)
- 1 tablespoon Blogilates Sculpt + Debloat Chocolate Shake Protein Powder
- 1½ tablespoons cocoa powder
- ½ teaspoon vanilla extract

Method

1. Blend all ingredients in a blender for 20 seconds.

2. Pour into a small pot over medium-high heat and whisk until piping hot.

Calories: 148 | Protein: 20g | Fat: 3g | Carbs: 35g | Fiber: 6g | Net-Carbs: 5g

Spoonable Chunky monkey Shake

"I wanted a super thick shake that could be eaten with a spoon, so I created this one with delicious chunks of goodness. But if you prefer to gulp it down, just blend instead of pulsing to incorporate everything until it's smooth and creamy."

Yield: 1 serving
Serving Size: 1 shake
Prep Time: 3 min

Ingredients

- 1 cup non-dariy milk
- 1 scoop Blogilates Sculpt + Deboat Sweet
    Cream Protein Powder
- 3/4 -1 cup ice
- 1 large frozen banana, sliced
- 2 tablespoon chopped walnuts
- 1 tablespoon sugar-free chocolate chips
- 1/4 cup freeze-dried bananas (optional)

Method

1. Place the milk, frozen banana, protein powder, and ice into a high-powered blender. Process until thick and smooth. Pulse in walnuts, chocolate chips, and freeze-dried bananas.

2. Pour into a glass and enjoy with a spoon or extra wide straw.

Calories: 384| Protein: 14g | Fat: 15g | Carbs: 55g | Fiber: 9g | Net-Carbs: 41g

Chai Smoothie

"This has all the spices and goodness of a hot chai tea, but gets a cool and creamy makeover as a quick, easy, and delicious smoothie."

Yield: 1 serving
Serving Size: 1 smoothie
Prep Time: 3 min

Ingredients

- ½ cup brewed and chilled chai tea*
- ½ cup non-dairy milk
- ¾ cup ice
- ½ small ripe banana
- 1 scoop Blogilates Sculpt + Debloat Sweet
    Cream Protein Powder
- 1 tablespoon granular monk fruit sweetener
- ¼ teaspoon nutmeg
- ¼ teaspoon cinnamon
- Pinch ground cloves

Method

1. Add all ingredients to a high-powered blender and process until thick and creamy (about 30 seconds).

2. *We suggest microwaving your favorite chai tea bag in ½ cup of water and placing in the fridge for an hour or overnight. When ready to make your shake, remove the tea bag and pour liquid into the blender.

Calories: 118 | Protein: 9g | Fat: 2g | Carbs: 29g | Fiber: 4g | Net-Carbs: 13g

Almond Blueberry Shake

"The magic of this shake comes from the dash of almond extract, which adds a distinct and special flavor. But if you don't have any, sub in vanilla extract instead."

Yield: 1 serving
Serving Size: 1 shake
Prep Time: 3 min

Ingredients

- 1 cup non-dairy milk
- 1 scoop Blogilates Sculpt + Debloat Sweet
    Cream Protein Powder
- ½ cup ice
- ½ cup frozen blueberries
- 1 tablespoon almond butter
- ½ teaspoon almond extract

Method

1. Add all ingredients to a blender and process until smooth and creamy.

Calories: 247 | Protein: 13g | Fat: 12g | Carbs: 24g | Fiber: 7g | Net-Carbs: 16g

Birthday Cake Shake

"I PROMISE you won't taste the cauliflower in this! Trust me- ok?! It adds amazing creaminess, ups the nutritional value, and might just become your secret added ingredient in every shake you ever make again."

Yield: 1 serving
Serving Size: 1 shake
Prep Time: 3 min

Ingredients

- 1¼ cups non-dairy milk
- 1 scoop Blogilates Sculpt + Debloat Sweet Cream Protein Powder
- ½ cup ice
- ½ frozen banana
- ⅓ cup frozen riced cauliflower*
- 2 tablespoons granular monk fruit sweetener
- ½ teaspoon vanilla extract
- 2 teaspoons sprinkles, divided**

Method

1. Add all ingredients except sprinkles to a high-powered blender and process until smooth.

2. Stir in sprinkles and serve.

3. *Frozen cauliflower is sold at most grocery stores. If you make your own, be sure to steam it, then freeze. It's undetectable in recipes and adds fiber, antioxidants and a creamy texture.

4. **There are several grocery stores and online retailers that carry sprinkles with no artificial coloring.

Calories: 207 | Protein: 11g | Fat: 5g | Carbs: 53g | Fiber: 5g | Net-Carbs: 24g

Chocolate Peanut Butter Shake

"I had to include one of the most beloved flavor combos of all time: chocolate, peanut butter and banana. It's always a home run."

Yield: 1 serving
Serving Size: 1 shake
Prep Time: 3 min

Ingredients

- 1 cup non-dairy milk
- 1 scoop Blogilates Sculpt + Debloat Chocolate Shake Protein Powder
- ½ frozen banana
- ½ — ¾ cup ice
- 1 tablespoon cocoa powder
- 1 tablespoon powdered monk fruit sweetener
- 1 tablespoon peanut butter
- 1 tablespoon crushed peanuts (optional)

Method

1. Add all ingredients except peanuts to a blender and process until smooth and thick. Stir in crushed peanuts if you like some crunch, and serve.

Calories: 315 | Protein: 16g | Fat: 17g | Carbs: 40g | Fiber: 8g | Net-Carbs: 21g

Peaches & Sweet Cream Shake

"With a Sweet Cream protein powder flavor, I just had to create a Peaches & Cream flavored shake! Uh-oh, now I can't get the song out of my head..."

Yield: 1 serving
Serving Size: 1 shake
Prep Time: 3 min

Ingredients

- 1 cup non-dairy milk
- 1 scoop Blogilates Sculpt + Debloat Sweet Cream Protein Powder
- 1 cup frozen peaches
- 2-3 ice cubes
- 1 tablespoon granular monk fruit sweetener
- ½ teaspoon vanilla extract (optional)

Method

1. Add everything to a blender and process until smooth and creamy, adjusting the ice to suit your desired thickness.

Calories: 152 | Protein: 10g | Fat: 3g | Carbs: 34g | Fiber: 6g | Net-Carbs: 16g

Pumpkin Pie Smoothie

"This tastes like fall in a glass! If you like 'pumpkin everything,' then you need this recipe in your life ASAP!"

Yield: 1 serving
Serving Size: 1 shake
Prep Time: 3 min

Ingredients

- 1 cup non-dairy milk
- 1 scoop Blogilates Sculpt + Debloat Sweet Cream Protein Powder
- 1 cup ice
- 1 sheet gluten-free graham cracker, crushed and divided
- 2 tablespoons canned pumpkin
- 2 tablespoons granular monk fruit sweetener
- ½ teaspoon pumpkin pie spice

Method

1. Add everything to a blender except a tablespoon of graham cracker crumbs and process until smooth and creamy. Top with reserved crumbs and serve.

Calories: 192 | Protein: 10g | Fat: 7g | Carbs: 46g | Fiber: 4g | Net-Carbs: 18g

Piña Colada Shake

"I always order virgin piña coladas when I'm on a tropical vacation. I don't think I've ever not!? Sipping on this feels like you're in Hawaii lounging by the pool...except, make it high protein."

Yield: 1 serving
Serving Size: 1 shake
Prep Time: 3 min

Ingredients

- 1 cup carton coconut milk (or other non-dairy milk)
- 1 scoop Blogilates Sculpt + Debloat Sweet Cream Protein Powder
- ½ cup ice
- ¾ cup frozen pineapple tidbits
- 1 tablespoon powdered monk fruit sweetener*
- 2 tablespoons shredded coconut
- ½ teaspoon coconut extract (optional)
- ¼ small frozen banana (optional)**

Method

1. Add everything to a blender and process until smooth and creamy.

*For a sweeter shake, use 2 tablespoons.

**Adding this small piece of frozen banana makes an even creamier shake without imparting a lot of banana flavor. This is only optional.

Calories: 251 | Protein: 10g | Fat: 11g | Carbs: 42g | Fiber: 7g | Net-Carbs: 23g

Mint Chip Shake

Yield: 1 serving
Serving Size: 1 shake
Prep Time: 3 min

Ingredients

- 1 cup non-dairy milk
- 1 scoop Blogilates Sculpt + Debloat Chocolate Shake Protein Powder
- 1 cup ice
- 1½ tablespoons granular monk fruit sweetener
- 2 tablespoons sugar-free chocolate chips
- ½ teaspoon peppermint extract

Method

1. Add all ingredients to a blender and process until smooth and creamy.

Calories: 177 | Protein: 10g | Fat: 9g | Carbs: 32g | Fiber: 5g | Net-Carbs: 5g

Chocolate Mocha Shake

"Even though I'm not a coffee lover, I know most people don't start their days without it. This is why I just had to make sure I included a java recipe that's just as good as your local cafe and gives you the morning jolt that gets ya going!"

Yield: 1 serving
Serving Size: 1 shake
Prep Time: 3 min

Ingredients

- ½ cup chilled coffee or espresso
- ½ cup non-dairy milk
- 1 scoop Blogilates Sculpt + Debloat Chocolate Shake Protein Powder
- ¾ — 1 cup ice
- 2 tablespoons powdered granular monk fruit sweetener
- 5 espresso beans (optional)

Method

1. Add all ingredients to a blender and process until smooth and creamy, adding the amount of ice needed to suit your desired consistency.

Calories: 76 | Protein: 9g | Fat: 1g | Carbs: 17g | Fiber: 3g | Net-Carbs: 3g

Chocolate Covered
Raspberry

"Raspberries are one of my favorite fruits, and they pair perfectly with chocolate. However, if you're not a chocolate person, try this one with my 'Sweet Cream' flavor instead."

Yield: 1 serving
Serving Size: 1 shake
Prep Time: 3 min

Ingredients

- 1 cup non-dairy milk
- 1 scoop Blogilates Sculpt + Debloat Chocolate Shake Protein Powder
- 1 tablespoon granular monk fruit sweetener
- ¾ cup frozen raspberries
- 2-4 ice cubes
- 2 tablespoons sugar-free chocolate chips

Method

1. Add all ingredients to a blender except the chocolate chips. Process until smooth. Pulse in the chocolate chips, and serve.

Calories: 280 | Protein: 12g | Fat: 10g | Carbs: 55g | Fiber: 13g | Net-Carbs: 21g

Break-fast

Blueberry Crepes

"Yes, you can have deliciously satisfying protein crepes on the table in less than 10 minutes. The syrupy blueberries are to die for in this recipe."

Yield: 1 serving
Serving Size: 1 crepe
Prep Time: 4 min
Cook Time: 5 min

Ingredients

- 1 scoop Blogilates Sculpt + Debloat Sweet Cream Protein Powder
- ½ cup liquid egg whites
- 3 tablespoons non-dairy milk
- 1 tablespoon tapioca flour
- ¼ cup frozen blueberries
- 1 tablespoon granular monk fruit sweetener
- Powdered monk fruit sweetener (optional)

Method

1. Add the protein powder, egg whites, milk, and tapioca flour to a small blender and process until smooth.

2. Lightly grease a crepe pan or medium-sized non-stick skillet over medium heat.

3. Pour batter into the pan and swirl to coat the bottom. Cook for almost 2 minutes, or until golden and nearly cooked through, then loosen sides and carefully flip, cooking for an additional minute.

4. Meanwhile, add the blueberries and sweetener to a small pot and heat over medium-high heat. Stir occasionally for 3 minutes to create a quick compote.

5. Remove the crepe to a plate, pour in the blueberries (which will be warm, soft, and syrupy), fold, and serve. If you'd like, sprinkle with powdered monk fruit sweetener.

Calories: 206 | Protein: 19g | Fat: 2g | Carbs: 43g | Fiber: 5g | Net-Carbs: 20g

Quick
Waffles

"Be sure to start by heating up your waffle iron, because by the time it's warm, your batter will be ready to go—it's that easy!"

Yield: 1 serving
Serving Size: 1 waffle
Prep Time: 5 min
Cook Time: 4 min

Ingredients

- nonstick cooking spray
- 1 scoop Blogilates Sculpt + Debloat Sweet
    Cream Protein Powder
- 3 tablespoons fine almond flour
- 1 egg
- 2 tablespoons non-dairy milk
- 1 tablespoon granular monk fruit sweetener
- 2 teaspoons melted coconut oil
- 1 teaspoon vanilla extract
- ½ teaspoon cinnamon
- ½ teaspoon baking powder
- ¼ teaspoon baking soda

Method

1. Heat a waffle iron and coat lightly with cooking spray.

2. Whisk all ingredients together until smooth. Pour into the waffle iron and cook according to manufacturer's directions (about 3-4 minutes) or until golden.

3. Top with your favorite fruit, syrup, nut butter, or additional monk fruit sweetener.

Calories: 349 | Protein: 19g | Fat: 25g | Carbs: 22g | Fiber: 5g | Net-Carbs: 5g

Vanilla
Protein
Pancakes

"I kept these super simple for you so that you can dress up the flavor with your favorite toppings, fruit, or syrup. You can also swap out the sweet cream protein for chocolate, if you like."

Yield: 2 servings
Serving Size: 4 pancakes
Prep Time: 5 min
Cook Time: 7 min

Ingredients

- 2 scoops Blogilates Sculpt + Debloat Sweet
    Cream Protein Powder
- ½ cup fine almond flour
- 1 tablespoon monk fruit sweetener
- ¼ cup non-dairy milk
- 2 eggs
- ½ teaspoon vanilla extract
- ½ teaspoon baking powder
- nonstick cooking spray

Method

1. Combine the protein powder, almond flour, and baking powder in a medium bowl.

2. Whisk in the milk, eggs, and vanilla extract until completely smooth.

3. Grease a griddle or large pan with butter, oil, or non-stick cooking spray over medium heat.

4. Using a scant ¼-cup measure, create 8 silver dollar sized pancakes.

5. Cook for about 2 minutes, or until small bubbles form. Flip when golden and cook for 1 additional minute.

6. Top with your favorite healthy syrup, fresh berries, or nut butter.

Calories: 295 | Protein: 20g | Fat: 20g | Carbs: 16g | Fiber: 5g | Net-Carbs: 5g

Supersculpt
Protein
Pancakes

"I ate this pretty much every day on my 90 day journey to muscle! Not only are the macros insane but it's so light and fluffy. It's the best protein pancake you will EVER eat."

Yield: 1 serving
Serving Size: 6 pancakes
Prep Time: 3 min
Cook Time: 3 min

Ingredients

- 2 scoops Blogilates Sculpt + Debloat Chocolate Shake Protein Powder (or sub Blogilates Sculpt + Debloat Sweet Cream Protein Powder)
- ⅓ cup liquid egg whites
- 1 tablespoon water
- 1 tablespoon tapioca flour
- ½ teaspoon baking powder
- nonstick cooking spray

Method

1. Whisk all ingredients until smooth.

2. Heat a griddle or large nonstick pan over medium heat and coat with cooking spray.

3. Pour batter into 6 circles by the heaping tablespoon and cook for 1-2 minutes (until bubbles start to form), then flip and cook for 30-second to 1 minute, or until golden and cooked through.

4. Top with fresh fruit, nut butter, monk fruit syrup or powdered monk fruit sweetener.

Calories: 182 | Protein: 25g | Fat: 0g | Carbs: 14g | Fiber: 5g | Net-Carbs: 10g

Cocoa Banana Baked Oats

"Sometimes a single serving is all you need, which is why this one is perfect if you live alone or don't need a bunch of leftovers."

Yield: 1 serving
Serving Size: full recipe
Prep Time: 3 min
Cook Time: 24 min

Ingredients

- nonstick cooking spray
- ½ very ripe medium banana
- ½ cup rolled oats
- 1 scoop Blogilates Sculpt + Debloat Chocolate Shake Protein Powder
- 1 tablespoon granular monk fruit sweetener
- ½ cup non-dairy milk*
- ¼ teaspoon baking soda

Method

1. Heat oven to 350°F. Mash banana with a fork in a medium bowl.

2. Add the rest of the ingredients and mix well.

3. Coat an oven-safe ramekin with cooking spray, pour in batter and bake for 22-26 minutes, or until set to your desired texture (less time for gooey, more time for firm).

4. Top with nut butter, powdered monk fruit or low-sugar syrup.

*For a firmer baked oatmeal, use ⅓ cup. For a more traditional bowl of oatmeal, use ½ cup.

Calories: 279 | Protein: 14g | Fat: 4g | Carbs: 58g | Fiber: 8g | Net-Carbs: 38g

Apple Spice Overnight Oats

Yield: 2 servings
Serving Size: 1 jar
Prep Time: 5 min
Chill Time: overnight

Ingredients

- 1 medium apple, finely chopped
- 3 tablespoons granular monk fruit sweetener
- 1 cup rolled oats
- 1 scoop Blogilates Sculpt + Debloat Sweet Cream Protein Powder
- 1 cup non-dairy milk
- ¼ cup applesauce
- 1 tablespoon ground flax
- 2 teaspoons cinnamon
- 1 teaspoon vanilla extract (optional)

Method

1. Stir the apple and monk fruit together in a medium bowl until well combined. Add in the oats, protein powder, milk, applesauce, flax, cinnamon, and vanilla and stir to combine.

2. Divide into 2 mason jars, cover with lids and refrigerate overnight.

Calories: 306 | Protein: 15g | Fat: 5g | Carbs: 69g | Fiber: 11g | Net-Carbs: 39g

PB & J
Oats

"Warm, cozy and the perfect pre- or post-workout meal! Full of energy and protein, these oats will leave you satisfied for hours."

Yield: 1 serving
Serving Size: full recipe
Prep Time: 3 min
Cook Time: 5 min

Ingredients

- ⅔ — ¾ cup non-dairy milk*
- ½ cup rolled oats
- 1 scoop Blogilates Sculpt + Debloat Sweet
     Cream Protein Powder*
- 1 tablespoon ground flax
- 2 tablespoon granular monk fruit sweetener
- 1 tablespoon peanut butter
- 1 tablespoon low-sugar jelly

Method

1. Add the milk, oats, protein powder, flax, and sweetener to a medium pot and heat the stovetop for 5 minutes or until thick and hot. (Alternatively, you can cook for 2 minutes in a microwave). Adjust the amount of milk to suit your desired texture and thickness.

2. Transfer to a bowl and swirl in the peanut butter and jelly.

*You can substitute Blogilates Sculpt + Debloat Chocolate Shake Protein Powder, if you prefer.

Calories: 387 | Protein: 19g | Fat: 15g | Carbs: 68g | Fiber: 9g | Net-Carbs: 36g

Strawberry
Vanilla
Baked
Oatmeal

"I love this recipe because you can grab a piece in a hurry, use it for meal prep, or share it with friends and family."

Yield: 9 servings
Serving Size: 1 baked oatmeal square
Prep Time: 5 min
Cookl Time: 28 min

Ingredients

- nonstick cooking spray
- 2 cups rolled oats
- 2 scoops Blogilates Sculpt + Debloat Sweet
   Cream Protein Powder
- ½ cup granular monk fruit sweetener
- 1 teaspoon cinnamon
- 1 teaspoon baking powder
- 1¾ cups non-dairy milk
- 1 egg
- 1 teaspoon vanilla extract
- 1 cup chopped strawberries
- ¼ cup sugar-free chocolate chips (optional)

Method

1. Heat oven to 350°. Coat a 9-by-9-inch baking dish with cooking spray.

2. Whisk together the oats, protein powder, sweetener, cinnamon, and baking powder in a medium bowl.

3. Stir in the milk, egg, and vanilla. Fold in the strawberries and chocolate chips, if using. Pour into the prepared pan and bake for 26-28 minutes, or until set. Cool 10 minutes before cutting into 9 squares.

Note: These oatmeal squares are delicious with a drizzle of drippy peanut butter on top. Yum!

Calories: 121 | Protein: 5g | Fat: 3g | Carbs: 29g | Fiber: 3g | Net-Carbs: 13g

Cinnamon Rolls

Yield: 10 servings
Serving Size: 1 cinnamon roll
Prep Time: 15 min
Cook Time: 12 min

Ingredients

Dough:
- 2 cups oat flour
- 2 scoops Blogilates Sculpt + Debloat Sweet Cream Protein Powder
- 1 teaspoon baking powder
- Pinch salt
- 3 tablespoons monk fruit syrup (or another low sugar syrup)
- 3-4 tablespoons unsweetened applesauce
- 1 egg
- ½ teaspoon vanilla extract
- nonstick cooking spray

Filling:
- ¼ cup monk fruit syrup (or another low sugar syrup)
- 3 tablespoons granular monk fruit sweetener
- 1 tablespoon cinnamon
- ¼ cup chopped walnuts

Icing:
- 2 tablespoons melted coconut butter*

"I remember going to the mall and BEGGING my mom to buy me a Cinnabon. I think maybe once she bought one for me and my sister to share. This recipe is for little Cassey."

Method

1. Heat oven to 350°F. Whisk together the oat flour, protein powder, baking powder, and salt.

2. Add the syrup, applesauce, egg, and vanilla and stir, then knead with hands, as dough will be thick.

3. Separate dough into two equal balls and place each between two sheets of parchment paper sprayed with cooking spray. Roll out into two rectangles.

4. Stir filling ingredients together and spoon across each dough. Gently roll from the long side, then cut each one into 5 pinwheels for a total of 10.

5. Nestle the rolled dough circles into a loaf pan. Bake for 12 minutes. Remove from oven and drizzle with coconut butter.

6. *An alternative drizzle to coconut butter is butter, syrup, or powdered monk fruit sweetener.

Calories: 93 | Protein: 4g | Fat: 4g | Carbs: 16g | Fiber: 4g | Net-Carbs: 8g

Muffins, Breads & Crusts

Dark Chocolate Donuts

Double Chocolate Muffins

Zucchini Muffins

Pumpkin Spice Muffins

Banana Bread

Low-Carb Sandwich Bread

Cauliflower Collagen Pizza Crust

Quick Carrot Loaf

Single-Serving Zucchini Bread

Dark Chocolate Donuts

"Honestly, it's donut shop worthy. Rich, soft, sweet, your taste buds will fall madly in love."

Yield: 6 servings
Serving Size: 1 donut
Prep Time: 5 min
Cook Time: 20 min

Ingredients

- 1 cup fine almond flour
- 3 scoops Blogilates Sculpt + Debloat Chocolate Shake Protein Powder
- ⅓ cup powdered monk fruit sweetener + ½ tablespoons
- 1 tablespoon dark cocoa powder
- ½ teaspoon baking powder
- ¼ teaspoon baking soda
- Pinch salt
- ⅔ cup non-dairy milk
- 1 egg, room temperature
- 2 tablespoons melted coconut oil, butter, or ghee
- 1 teaspoon vanilla extract

Method

1. Heat oven to 350°F. Add the almond flour, protein powder, ⅓ cup sweetener, cocoa powder, baking powder, baking soda, and salt to a medium bowl and whisk to combine.

2. Whisk in the milk, egg, oil, and vanilla.

3. Spoon batter into 6 silicone donut molds. Bake for about 20 minutes, or until an inserted toothpick comes out clean.

4. Cool completely before carefully inverting the donuts onto a plate. Sift remaining ½ tablespoon sweetener on top and serve.

Calories: 196 | Protein: 9g | Fat: 15g | Carbs: 14g | Fiber: 3g | Net-Carbs: 3g

Double Chocolate Muffins

"This one-bowl wonder muffin recipe couldn't be any easier! Feel free to sub in another type of nut butter, if you like."

Yield: 8 servings
Serving Size: 1 muffin
Prep Time: 5 min
Cook Time: 15 min

Ingredients

- ¾ cup drippy cashew butter
- 3 eggs
- 1 tablespoon melted coconut oil, ghee, or butter
- 1 scoop Blogilates Sculpt + Debloat Chocolate Shake Protein Powder
- 2 tablespoons cocoa powder
- ½ teaspoon baking powder
- Pinch salt
- ¼ cup sugar-free chocolate chips (optional)

Method

1. Heat oven to 350°F. Whisk the cashew butter, eggs, and oil together.

2. Add the protein powder, cocoa powder, baking powder, and salt and stir to form a thick batter. Fold in chocolate chips, if using.

3. Spoon batter into 8 silicone muffin cups and bake for 14-15 minutes. If you like a gooey center, slightly underbake.

Calories: 216 | Protein: 8g | Fat: 17g | Carbs: 11g | Fiber: 2g | Net-Carbs: 7g

Zucchini Muffins

"You get fruit and veggies in this simple recipe that makes enough for you to freeze some for later (if they last that long)."

Yield: 12 servings
Serving Size: 1 muffin
Prep Time: 10 min
Cook Time: 30 min

Ingredients

- 1 large zucchini
- Pinch salt
- 1 cup fine oat flour
- 2 scoops Blogilates Sculpt + Debloat Sweet Cream Protein Powder
- ½ cup granular monk fruit sweetener
- ½ cup unsweetened applesauce
- ¼ cup drippy almond butter
- 2 large eggs
- 1¼ teaspoons baking powder
- ¼ cup sugar-free chocolate chips (optional)

Method

1. Heat oven to 350°F. Grate the zucchini and sprinkle with salt. Let sit for 5 minutes. Squeeze out the liquid with a tea towel, then place the zucchini shreds into a mixing bowl.

2. In a separate bowl, whisk the oat flour, protein powder, and sweetener.

3. Add the applesauce, almond butter, and eggs to the bowl with the zucchini. Add the dry ingredients with the baking powder and chocolate chips.

4. Spoon batter into 12 silicone muffin cups. Bake for 22-23 minutes or until an inserted toothpick comes out clean.

Calories: 137 | Protein: 7g | Fat: 7g | Carbs: 25g | Fiber: 3g | Net-Carbs: 10g

Pumpkin Spice Muffins

"Fall flavors burst out of these soft, festive pumpkin muffins!"

Yield: 8 servings
Serving Size: 1 muffin
Prep Time: 5 min
Cook Time: 24 min

Ingredients

- ¾ cup almond flour
- 2 scoops Blogilates Sculpt + Debloat Sweet Cream Protein Powder
- 1 cup canned pumpkin puree
- ½ cup granular monk fruit sweetener
- 2 eggs
- 2 teaspoons pumpkin pie spice
- 1 teaspoon baking powder

Method

1. Heat oven to 350°F.

2. Whisk all ingredients in a medium bowl. Spoon batter into 8 silicone muffin cups and bake for 22-24 minutes or until an inserted toothpick comes out clean.

Calories: 85 | Protein: 5g | Fat: 5g | Carbs: 14g | Fiber: 2g | Net-Carbs: 3g

Banana Bread

"Banana bread will always have a special place in my heart. It helped calm me in a time of uncertainty and ignited my passion for a skill that has always intimidated me: baking."

Yield: 10 servings
Serving Size: 1 slice
Prep Time: 10 min
Cook Time: 42 min

Ingredients

- nonstick cooking spray
- 2 large ripe bananas
- 2 eggs
- ⅔ cup non-dairy milk
- 1 tablespoon melted coconut oil, ghee, or butter
- 1½ cups oat flour
- 2 scoops Blogilates Sculpt + Debloat Sweet Cream Protein Powder
- ½ cup granular monk fruit sweetener
- 2 teaspoons baking powder
- ¼ teaspoon salt
- ¼ cup sugar-free chocolate chips (optional)

Method

1. Heat oven to 350°F. Line a 9-by-5-inch loaf pan with parchment paper. Spray lightly with cooking spray.

2. Mash the bananas in a medium bowl (or feel free to blend them with the eggs and milk to be completely "chunk-free"). Add the eggs, milk, and oil and whisk to combine.

3. In a separate bowl, whisk the oat flour, protein powder, sweetener, baking powder, and salt. Add to the wet ingredients and stir to combine. Add the chocolate chips. Pour batter into the prepared pan and bake for 42-44 minutes or until an inserted toothpick comes out clean. If you like your baked goods slightly underdone, choose the lesser cooking time.

Calories: 150 | Protein: 6g | Fat: 5g | Carbs: 32g | Fiber: 3g | Net-Carbs: 17g

Low-Carb Sandwich Bread

"I'm always on the hunt for a low-carb bread that I can toast and slather a topping on. This one comes together quickly and is pretty close to the real thing!"

Yield: 14 servings
Serving Size: 1 slice
Prep Time: 5 min
Cook Time: 38 min

Ingredients

- nonstick cooking spray
- 1 cup liquid egg whites
- 1 cup drippy almond butter
- 3 large eggs
- 2 scoops Blogilates Sculpt + Debloat Sweet Cream Protein Powder
- ¼ cup coconut flour
- 1½ tablespoons apple cider vinegar
- 2 teaspoons baking soda
- ¼ teaspoon sea salt

Method

1. Heat oven to 325°F. Line a 9-x-5-inch loaf pan with parchment paper and spray lightly with cooking spray.

2. Place the egg whites, almond butter, and egg into a blender and process on low for 20 seconds, or until combined.

3. Add in the protein powder, coconut flour, vinegar, baking soda, and salt. Process again on medium-low for 20 seconds.

4. Pour batter into prepared loaf pan and bake for 38-40 minutes, or until an inserted toothpick comes out clean.

5. Remove from pan to a wire rack. Cool before cutting into 14 slices. Wrap any unused portions and store in the fridge for 4 days or in the freezer. Pop into the toaster for quick toast!

Calories: 151 | Protein: 8g | Fat: 11g | Carbs: 5g | Fiber: 3g | Net-Carbs: 2g

Cauliflower Collagen Pizza Crust

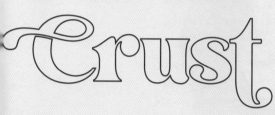

> "I love pizza but rarely make it from scratch because it usually takes a long time, or, kinda falls apart. But not this recipe! It's sturdier than most cauli-crusts and super easy to make."

Yield: 8 servings
Serving Size: 1 slice
Prep Time: 10 min
Cook Time: 24 min

Ingredients

- 2 cups frozen riced cauliflower, defrosted
- 1 egg
- 4 scoops Blogilates Beauty Collagen Peptides
- 1 cup dairy-free shredded cheese
- ½ teaspoon Italian seasoning
- ¼ teaspoon sea salt
nonstick cooking spray

Method

1. Heat oven to 400°F. Squeeze all liquid out of the defrosted riced cauliflower using a nut bag or tea towel, then place into a food processor.

2. Add the egg and collagen powder and process until almost smooth. Pulse in the cheese, Italian seasoning, and salt.

3. Coat a piece of parchment paper with cooking spray and place onto a baking sheet. Pour the crust batter in the center, forming a large dinner plate size circle using the back of a spoon.

4. Bake for 12 minutes. Remove from oven, and using a spatula, separate the crust from any sticky parts of the parchment paper. Carefully flip, or invert onto a second sheet of parchment. Return to the baking sheet and oven and bake for another 10-12 minutes or until golden and firm.

5. Reduce the oven heat to 350°F, top with your favorite sauce and cheese, and bake your pizza for about 10 minutes.

Calories: 83 | Protein: 7g | Fat: 4g | Carbs: 4g | Fiber: 1g | Net-Carbs: 4g

Quick Carrot Loaf

"Carrot cake, in bread form. Literally so good."

Yield: 10 servings
Serving Size: 1 slice
Prep Time: 5 min
Cook Time: 28 min

Ingredients

- 1¼ cups almond flour
- ¼ cup granular monk fruit sweetener
- 2 scoops Blogilates Sculpt + Debloat Sweet
    Cream Protein Powder
- 1 teaspoon pumpkin pie spice
- ¾ teaspoon baking soda
- ¼ teaspoon salt
- 2 eggs
- 1 egg white
- 2 tablespoons unsweetened applesauce
- ¾ cup shredded carrots
- ¼ cup chopped walnuts, optional

Method

1. Heat oven to 350°F. Line an 8½-by-4½ loaf pan with parchment paper and lightly spray it with cooking spray.

2. Whisk the dry ingredients (almond flour, sweetener, protein powder, pumpkin pie spice, baking soda, and salt) in a medium bowl.

3. Whisk in the eggs, egg white, and applesauce. Fold in the carrots and walnuts, if using.

4. Pour into the prepared pan and bake for 27-28 minutes or until an inserted toothpick comes out clean.

Calories: 130 | Protein: 7g | Fat: 10g | Carbs: 10g | Fiber: 1g | Net-Carbs: 2g

Single-Serving Zucchini Bread

"Made this while playing around in the kitchen with all the extra zucchini I had laying around! I ate this a lot on my 90 Day Journey. It was perfect for dessert."

Yield: 1 serving
Serving Size: full recipe
Prep Time: 15 min
Cook Time: 22 min

Ingredients

- nonstick cooking spray
- 1 small zucchini
- ½ teaspoon salt
- 1½ scoops Blogilates Sculpt + Debloat Sweet
      Cream Protein Powder
- 1 egg
- 3 tablespoons granular monk fruit sweetener
- 1 tablespoon tapioca flour
- ½ teaspoon baking powder
- Cinnamon and chocolate chips on top
(optional)

Method

1. Heat oven to 350°F. Grate the zucchini, sprinkle with salt, and let sit for 5-10 minutes to draw out the moisture. Squeeze out the liquid in a clean tea towel or nut bag.

2. Add the zucchini to a medium bowl with the remaining ingredients and whisk until fully combined.

3. Coat a large ramekin with cooking spray and pour in the batter.

4. Bake for 26-29 minutes, or until set. (Alternatively, microwave it for 2 minutes and 30 seconds, or until set).

5. Feel free to add cinnamon or sugar-free chocolate chips too!

Calories: 200 | Protein: 20g | Fat: 6g | Carbs: 51g | Fiber: 4g | Net-Carbs: 11g

Quick Snac

Nutty Granola

Hawaiian Bliss Bites

Cinnamon Roll Bites

Maple Cinnamon Protein Bars

Protein Popcorn

Carrot Cake Bites

Protein Cookie Dough

Peanut Butter Protein Balls

Collagen Coconut Cashew Butter

Nutty Granola

"When I have snacks like this on hand I never get 'hangry.' This granola is great on its own, or tossed into some non-dairy yogurt."

Yield: 8 servings
Serving Size: ¼ cup
Prep Time: 5 min
Cook Time: 16 min

Ingredients

- ¼ cup drippy almond butter
- ¼ cup low sugar syrup or honey
- 2 tablespoons coconut oil
- 2 cups mixed nuts
- 1 scoop Blogilates Sculpt + Debloat Sweet
  Cream Protein Powder
- ⅓ cup unsweetened flaked coconut
- 1 tablespoon ground flax
- 1 teaspoon vanilla extract
- 1 teaspoon cinnamon

Method

1. Heat oven to 325°F. Add the almond butter, syrup, and oil to a medium bowl and microwave for about 1 minute until melted. Stir well.

2. Mix the nuts, protein powder, coconut, and flax in a separate bowl. Add the wet to the dry and stir to coat. Add the vanilla and cinnamon and stir again.

3. Pour onto a baking sheet lined with parchment paper or a silicone mat and spread out. Bake for 8 minutes. Remove from oven to stir, then return to the oven for another 6-8 minutes, or until the nuts and coconut begin to brown.

4. Cool completely before storing.

Calories: 308 | Protein: 6g | Fat: 30g | Carbs: 8g | Fiber: 5g | Net-Carbs: 3g

Hawaiian Bliss Bites

"These cute little no-bake cookies taste like a tropical vacation in your mouth!"

Yield: 9 servings
Serving Size: 1 bliss bite
Prep Time: 5 min
Chill Time: 20 min

Ingredients

- nonstick cooking spray
- 1 cup salted macadamia nuts
- 1 cup shredded unsweetened coconut
- 3 scoops Blogilates Beauty Collagen Peptides
- 2 tablespoons honey
- 1 teaspoon coconut oil
- 1 teaspoon vanilla bean paste (optional)

Method

1. Pulse the nuts, coconut, and collagen peptides in a food processor to coarse crumbs. Pulse in remaining ingredients until it sticks together when pressed between your hands.

2. Coat a tablespoon with cooking spray, then by the heaping tablespoon, scoop out 9 uniform balls and press into the tablespoon creating rounded tops and flat bottoms. Refrigerate for 20 minutes before serving.

3. Store in the refrigerator.

Calories: 177 | Protein: 5g | Fat: 16g | Carbs: 8g | Fiber: 2g | Net-Carbs: 5g

Cinnamon Roll Bites

"I love these as a little pre- or post-workout snack. I just keep them in a container in the fridge when I need a little something sweet, yet light."

Yield: 10 servings
Serving Size: 1 cinnamon roll bite
Prep Time: 5 min

Ingredients

- ½ cup drippy cashew or almond butter (or sunflower butter)
- 1 scoop Blogilates Sculpt + Debloat Sweet Cream Protein Powder
- 3 tablespoons coconut flour
- 2 tablespoons monk fruit syrup
- 1½ teaspoons cinnamon, divided
- 1½ teaspoons granular monk fruit sweetener

Method

1. Stir together the nut butter, protein powder, coconut flour, syrup, and 1 teaspoon cinnamon in a medium bowl. Once it resembles thick dough, form 10 equal sized balls.

2. Add the remaining cinnamon and monk fruit to a bowl and coat each ball.

3. Store in the refrigerator.

Calories: 93 | Protein: 4g | Fat: 7g | Carbs: 8g | Fiber: 2g | Net-Carbs: 4g

Maple Cinnamon Protein Bars

"Who needs packaged bars when you have these?! They're a fun snack that fills you up with maple cinnamon goodness."

Yield: 8 servings
Serving Size: 1 bar
Prep Time: 10 min
Chill Time: 10 min

Ingredients

- 2 cups rolled oats
- 3 scoops Blogilates Sculpt + Debloat Sweet Cream Protein Powder (69 grams)
- ¾ cup drippy natural nut butter
- ½ cup sugar-free monk fruit maple syrup
- 2 teaspoons coconut oil
- 2 teaspoons cinnamon
- ¼ cup chopped nuts
- - Dark chocolate, melted (optional)

Method

1. Line a 9 x 5-inch loaf pan with parchment paper.

2. Add the oats and protein powder to a large bowl.

3. Combine the nut butter, syrup, and oil in a seperate bowl and microwave for 1 minute, stirring mid-way.

4. Stir nut butter mixture into the oats with cinnamon and nuts. Stir in nuts. Press into the pan and press firmly. Refrigerate for 30 minutes or until firm enough to cut.

5. If desired, drizzle with melted dark chocolate.

Calories: 285 | Protein: 11g | Fat: 18g | Carbs: 24g | Fiber: 7g | Net-Carbs: 15g

Protein
Popcorn

"The next time your besties come over for movie night, pop some of this protein popcorn and watch it disappear really fast. The salty-sweet combo is delicious."

Yield: 8 servings
Serving Size: 1 heaping cup
Prep Time: 3 min
Cook Time: 3 min

Ingredients

- 5 tablespoons ghee or butter -lavored coconut
    oil, divided
- ¾ cup popcorn kernels
- 2 scoops Blogilates Sculpt + Debloat
    Chocolate Shake Protein Powder
- 2 tablespoons powdered monk fruit sweetener
- 1 tablespoon cocoa powder
- Pinch of salt
- ¼ cup sugar-free chocolate chips (optional)

Additional Flavor Combinations:
- Blogilates Sculpt + Debloat Sweet Cream
    Protein Powder with either cinnamon or
    sugar-free white chocolate chips
- Blogilates Sculpt + Debloat Chocolate Shake
    Protein Powder with PB2 powder.

Method

1. Place 3 tablespoons of ghee/oil in a large 10L/10qt lightweight pot over medium heat.

2. When the ghee has almost melted, add kernels, shake quickly to spread across the base, then cover with the lid.

3. Shake briefly once after 30 seconds of popping. When the popping stops, immediately pour popcorn into a large bowl.

4. In a small bowl, mix together the protein powder, sweetener, cocoa, and salt.

5. Melt remaining ghee and toss into the popcorn. Sprinkle the powder mixture onto the popcorn and shake and stir to coat. Add in the chocolate chips, if using.

Calories: 149 | Protein: 4g | Fat: 8g | Carbs: 17g | Fiber: 3g | Net-Carbs: 10g

Carrot Cake Bites

"If you prefer to sweeten things 100% naturally, this recipe is for you. Not only do the carrots offer a bit of sweetness and texture, but the dates make these a chewy, delightful home-run."

Yield: 10 servings
Serving Size: 1 carrot cake bite
Prep Time: 10 min

Ingredients

- 12 medium-sized dates (about ⅔ cup)
- ¾ cup shredded carrots
- 2 scoops Blogilates Sculpt + Debloat Sweet Cream Protein Powder
- 3 tablespoons almond butter
- 2 tablespoons coconut flour
- 1 teaspoon cinnamon
- 2 tablespoons shredded coconut

Method

1. Add the dates to a food processor and process to small chunks. Add the carrots, protein powder, almond butter, coconut flour, and cinnamon and pulse until a dough forms.

2. Roll dough into 10 balls and coat with the coconut.

3. Store leftovers in the refrigerator.

Calories: 133 | Protein: 4g | Fat: 3g | Carbs: 25g | Fiber: 4g | Net-Carbs: 21g

Protein Cookie Dough

"Cookie dough is often a treat that's easy to overdo. That's why my version is the perfect serving size for one, and it's super healthy too."

Yield: 1 serving
Serving Size: about 1/3 cup dough
Prep Time: 5 min

Ingredients

- 1 scoop Blogilates Sculpt + Debloat Sweet
     Cream Protein Powder
- 2½-3 tablespoons non-dairy milk
- 2 tablespoons coconut flour
- 2 tablespoons granular monk fruit sweetener
- 1 tablespoon melted butter-flavored coconut
     oil (or butter or cashew butter)
- 1 teaspoon vanilla extract
- Pinch salt
- 1 tablespoon sugar-free chocolate chips

Method

1. Stir everything except the chocolate chips together to form a dough, adding the milk in a little at a time to reach the desired, soft consistency. Stir in the chocolate chips, and serve.

Calories: 231 | Protein: 12g | Fat: 11g | Carbs: 44g | Fiber: 8g | Net-Carbs: 7g

Peanut Butter Protein Balls

"These are so fast to make and so fun to eat. Perfectly packable for on-the-go as well!"

Yield: 6 servings
Serving Size: 1 protein ball
Prep Time: 5 min

Ingredients

- ½ cup peanut butter
- 2 scoops Vanilla or Chocolate Blogilates Sculpt + Debloat Protein Powder
- 2 tablespoons granular monk fruit sweetener
- ½ teaspoon vanilla extract
- Pinch salt
- 3 tablespoons crushed peanuts

Method

1. Stir together all ingredients except the crushed peanuts until a thick dough forms. Roll into balls and roll in the crushed peanuts. Store in the refrigerator.

Calories: 191 | Protein: 10g | Fat: 15g | Carbs: 11g | Fiber: 3g | Net-Carbs: 5g

Collagen Coconut Cashew Butter

"OMG. I am a cashew butter die-hard. Add in the coconut and I feel like I'm in Bora Bora all over again. Sam, we need Honeymoon 2.0 ASAP."

Yield: 8 servings
Serving Size: about 2 tablespoons
Prep Time: 5 min

Ingredients

- 1½ cups lightly salted cashew pieces
- 2 scoops Blogilates Beauty Collagen Peptides
- ¼ cup unsweetened coconut flakes
- 2 tablespoons granular monk fruit sweetener
- 1 tablespoon coconut oil

Method

1. Add everything to a high-powered blender or food processor and process until smooth (about 3 minutes), scraping sides as needed.

2. Store in the pantry for up to two weeks, or in the fridge for extended storage.

* Change up the flavor profile by omitting the coconut flakes and adding cocoa powder, sugar-free chocolate chips, cinnamon, or vanilla extract.

Calories: 188 | Protein: 6g | Fat: 15g | Carbs: 12g | Fiber: 1g | Net-Carbs: 8g

Dess-erts

Chocolate Chip Blondies

Low-Carb Brownies

Almond Happy Bites

Chocolate Silk Pudding

Vegan Vanilla Pudding

Freezer PB Cups

No-Bake Vegan Key Lime Cheesecake

Chocolate Walnut Chunk Cookie

Vegan Vanilla Date Cookies

Blueberry Crisp

Chocolate PB Mug Cake

Lemon Mug Cake

Chocolate Protein Fudge

Chocolate Cherry Chia Parfait

No-Churn Vanilla Protein Ice Cream

Mixed-Berry Protein Nice Cream

S'mores Cake Pops

Super Fluff Blender Ice Cream

Collagen Beauty Bark

Flourless Chocolate Torte

Berry Crumble Bars

Chocolate Chip Blondies

"These blondies are warm, soft squares of happiness to my soul. I make it with chocolate for Sam and without for me!"

Yield: 12 servings
Serving Size: 1 square
Prep Time: 10 min
Cook Time: 30 min

Ingredients

- nonstick cooking spray
- 1 (15-oz) can chickpeas, drained
- ⅔ cup granular monk fruit sweetener
- 4 scoops Blogilates Beauty Collagen Peptides*
- ⅓ cup nut butter
- 2 tablespoons almond flour
- 1½ teaspoons vanilla extract
- ½ teaspoon baking powder
- ¼ teaspoon baking soda
- ¼ teaspoon salt
- ⅓ cup sugar-free chocolate chips, divided

Method

1. Heat oven to 350°F. Coat an 8-by-8-inch baking dish with cooking spray.

2. Add everything but the chocolate chips to a food processor and process until smooth. Stir in half of the chocolate chips and pour into baking dish. Top with remaining chocolate chips.

3. Bake for 30 minutes or until set. If you like a gooey blondie, underbake a touch.

*To make this a vegan recipe, swap the collagen for 1½ scoops of Blogilates Sculpt + Debloat Sweet Cream Protein Powder.

Calories: 115 | Protein: 7g | Fat: 6g | Carbs: 22g | Fiber: 2g | Net-Carbs: 7g

Low-Carb Brownies

Yield: 10 servings
Serving Size: 1 brownie
Prep Time: 5 min
Cook Time: 25 min

Ingredients

- ½ cup coconut oil, or butter
- ½ cup sugar-free chocolate chips
- ⅔ cup almond flour
- 1 scoop Blogilates Sculpt + Debloat Chocolate Shake Protein Powder
- ⅓ cup granular monk fruit sweetener
- 2 eggs
- 1 teaspoon vanilla extract
- Pinch sea salt

Method

1. Heat oven to 350°F. Melt the oil and chocolate chips in the microwave in a glass bowl in 30-second increments, until smooth (about 2 minutes).

2. Whisk the almond flour, protein powder and sweetener in a separate bowl. Stir in the chocolate mixture, eggs and vanilla until smooth.

3. Pour into a greased 8-by-4-inch loaf pan. Sprinkle with sea salt. Bake for 20-22 minutes. Cool completely before cutting into 10 squares.

Calories: 196 | Protein: 4g | Fat: 18g | Carbs: 14g | Fiber: 2g | Net-Carbs: 2g

Almond Happy Bites

"Candy. But make it healthy. I also love a recipe that asks me to chill instead of bake. I just feel less anxious because I know it can't burn!"

Yield: 10 servings
Serving Size: 1 piece
Prep Time: 5 min
Cook Time: 2 min
Chill Time: 20 min

Ingredients

- ⅓ cup coconut butter
- 2½ tablespoons coconut oil
- ¾ cup finely shredded unsweetened coconut
- 1½ scoops Blogilates Beauty Collagen Peptides
- 3 tablespoons powdered monk fruit sweetener
- 1 teaspoon vanilla extract

Topping
- ⅓ cup sugar-free chocolate chips
- 1 teaspoon coconut oil
- 10 whole almonds

Method

1. Microwave the coconut butter and coconut oil in a microwave-safe bowl in 20-second intervals (about 1 minute) until smooth.

2. Stir in the coconut, collagen peptides, sweetener, and vanilla until fully combined.

3. Form 10 bite sized coconut mounds. Refrigerate for 10 minutes.

4. Meanwhile, microwave the chocolate chips and coconut oil in a small glass ramekin until smooth (about 90 seconds), stirring midway.

5. Fully coat each mound, top with an almond, and return to the fridge for 10 minutes, or until chocolate hardens. Store in a sealed container on the countertop for a softer candy.

Calories: 141 | Protein: 2g | Fat: 13g | Carbs: 9g | Fiber: 2g | Net-Carbs: 1g

Chocolate Silk Pudding

"Your taste buds will be shockingly delighted with how fatty, sweet, and chocolatey this is."

Yield: 2 servings
Serving Size: ½ recipe
Prep Time: 5 min
Chill Time: 2 hr

Ingredients

- ½ large, soft avocado
- 1 ripe banana
- 1 scoop Blogilates Sculpt + Debloat Chocolate Shake Protein Powder
- ¼ cup powdered monk fruit sweetener
- 1 tablespoon dark cocoa powder
- 2 teaspoons vanilla extract
- Pinch sea salt
- 1 tablespoon sugar-free chocolate chips (optional)
- Chopped strawberries or honey on top (optional)

Method

1. Add all ingredients to a blender and process until all chia seeds break down (the end result should resemble flax meal) and mixture is semi-smooth, about 30 seconds.

2. Pour into a glass bowl and refrigerate for a minimum of two hours to thicken up, resulting in a thick, creamy pudding with vanilla bean and chia flecks.

Calories: 175 | Protein: 6g | Fat: 7g | Carbs: 24g | Fiber: 6g | Net-Carbs: 15g

Vegan Vanilla Pudding

"This tastes like luxury. Seriously, the fattiness from the coconut milk and the fun chewy bits from the chia are a power combo."

Yield: 1 serving
Serving Size: full recipe
Prep Time: 5 min
Chill Time: 2 hrs

Ingredients

- ¾ cup canned lite coconut milk'
- 1 scoop Blogilates Sculpt + Debloat Sweet
    Cream Protein Powder
- 2 tablespoons chia seeds
- 2 tablespoons powdered monk fruit sweetener
- 1 teaspoon vanilla bean paste (or extract)

Method

1. Add all ingredients to a blender and process until all chia seeds have broken down and mixture is smooth, about 30 seconds.

2. Pour into a glass bowl and refrigerate for a minimum of two hours to thicken up.

3. Feel free to top with chopped strawberries or a drizzle of honey.

Calories: 275 | Protein: 12g | Fat: 16g | Carbs: 45g | Fiber: 9g | Net-Carbs: 12g

Freezer PB Cups

"I am obsessed with how much they look like "real" peanut butter cups from the store! The taste is *chef's kiss*"

Yield: 10 servings
Serving Size: 1 min cup
Prep Time: 10 min
Cook Time: 2 min
Freeze Time: 1 hr

Ingredients

- ½ cup drippy natural peanut butter
- 1 scoop Blogilates Sculpt + Debloat Sweet Cream Protein Powder
- 3 tablespoons non-dairy milk
- 2 tablespoons Powdered monk fruit Sweetener
- 1¼ cups sugar-free chocolate chips
- 1 teaspoon coconut oil
- Pinch sea salt

Method

1. Whisk together the peanut butter, protein powder, milk, and sweetener in a medium bowl until you reach a dough consistency.

2. Combine the chocolate chips and coconut oil in a separate bowl and microwave for about 2 minutes, stirring every 30 seconds, until smooth.

3. Using 10 silicone muffin molds (or paper molds), spoon about 1 tablespoon of chocolate into the base of each, coating slightly up the sides.

4. Take the peanut butter dough and roll into 10 balls, then flatten into disks the size of the base of the muffin cup. Gently press into the chocolate.

5. Cover each with remaining melted chocolate and sprinkle lightly with sea salt.

6. Freeze for 1 hour. Thaw slightly before enjoying.

Calories: 169 | Protein: 5g | Fat: 13g | Carbs: 19g | Fiber: 3g | Net-Carbs: 3g

No-Bake Vegan Key Lime Cheesecake

"I just died and went to cheesecake heaven."

Yield: 10 servings
Serving Size: 1 cheesecake
Prep Time: 20 min
Cook Time: 2 min
Freeze Time: 4 hrs

Ingredients

- 2 cups boiling water
- 1 cup raw cashew pieces
- 1 cup (about 18) pitted medium-sized dates, chopped
- 1 cup walnuts
- 3 scoops (69g) Blogilates Sculpt + Debloat Sweet Cream Protein Powder
- ½ cup granular monk fruit sweetener
- ¼ cup full-fat canned coconut milk
- Juice and zest from one large lime
- 1 tablespoon coconut oil

Method

1. Soak cashews in the water for 2 hours. Drain well. Set aside.

2. Pulse the dates in a blender or food processor, then add the walnuts and pulse to coarse crumbs.

3. Divide the crumbs into 10 muffin cups (we used silicone muffin cups) and press into the bottoms and slightly up the sides.

4. Blend the drained cashews, protein powder, sweetener, coconut milk (aim to use the creamed top part, if possible), lime zest and juice, and coconut oil in a blender or food processor and process until completely smooth.

5. Divide between all of the crusts. Freeze for 4 hours. Remove from muffin cups, and serve.

Calories: 254 | Protein: 7g | Fat: 16g | Carbs: 24g | Fiber: 4g | Net-Carbs: 20g

Chocolate Walnut Chunk Cookie

"Did you know I used to sell homemade cookies throughout middle school and high school? It was my first real business. The kids called em "crack cookies." They were legendary. I sold so many that the principal called me into the office and told me I had to stop."

Yield: 8 servings
Serving Size: 1 cookie
Prep Time: 5 min
Cook Time: 12 min

Ingredients

- ¾ cup almond flour
- ¼ cup nut or sunbutter*
- ¼ cup granular monk fruit sweetener
- 1 scoop Blogilates Sculpt + Debloat Chocolate Shake Protein Powder
- 3 tablespoons non-dairy milk
- 1 tablespoon cocoa powder
- 2 teaspoons melted coconut oil
- 2 tablespoons crushed walnuts
- 2 tablespoons sugar-free chocolate chips

Method

1. Heat oven to 350°F.

2. Stir everything together in a medium bowl. Prepare a baking sheet with parchment or a silicone baking mat. Form 8 balls and lightly press down. Bake for 12 minutes. Cool completely before enjoying.

*We used walnut butter, which you can buy or make by simply putting walnuts in a food processor and blending until smooth. Cashew butter has a neutral flavor too, which we also recommend.

Calories: 150 | Protein: 5g | Fat: 13g | Carbs: 12g | Fiber: 3g | Net-Carbs: 2g

Vegan Vanilla Date Cookies

"Dates make everything better. Speaking of... Sam and I need to make time for one. It's been a while."

Yield: 10 servings
Serving Size: 1 cookie
Prep Time: 5 min
Cook Time: 12 min

Ingredients

- 1½ cups soft pitted dates*
- ¾ cup dry oats
- 3 scoops Blogilates Sculpt + Debloat Sweet Cream Protein Powder
- ½ cup cashew butter (or sub almond or sun butter)
- 1 teaspoon vanilla extract
- Pinch salt
- ¼ cup sugar-free chocolate chips (optional)

Method

1. Heat oven to 350°F.

2. Process the dates in a food processor until smooth, then add in remaining ingredients (except chocolate chips, if using) and pulse several times until a dough is formed. Stir in chocolate chips, if desired.

3. By the heaping tablespoon, scoop out 10 portions and place on a parchment-lined baking sheet. Very gently press the top down (shape should still resemble a ball). Bake for 10-12 minutes or until the tops turn golden. Cool completely before removing from the baking sheet.

4. *If your dates are not super soft, soak them in very hot water for an hour, then drain completely.

Calories: 197 | Protein: 6g | Fat: 8g | Carbs: 29g | Fiber: 4g | Net-Carbs: 23g

Blueberry Crisp

"When I bite into this, I feel like I am laying in a meadow of light blue flowers wearing a simple white cotton dress, long grass blowing in the wind, a small wooden cottage in the distance."

Yield: 2 servings
Serving Size: ½ recipe
Prep Time: 5 min
Cook Time: 20 min

Ingredients

- 1 cup fresh blueberries
- 2 scoops Blogilates Beauty Collagen Peptides
- 3 tablespoons almond flour
- 2 tablespoons granular monk fruit sweetener
- 2 tablespoons softened butter flavored
     coconut oil, browned butter, ghee or butter
- 2 tablespoons chopped pecans or walnuts

Method

1. Heat oven to 350°F. Divide blueberries between two oven-safe ramekins.

2. Stir together the collagen, almond flour, sweetener, butter, and nuts to form a crumble. Divide over the top of the blueberries. Bake for 20 minutes.

Calories: 286 | Protein: 13g | Fat: 22g | Carbs: 26g | Fiber: 4g | Net-Carbs: 10g

Chocolate PB Mug Cake

Yield: 1 serving
Serving Size: 1 cake
Prep Time: 5 min
Cook Time: 2 min

Ingredients

- Nonstick cooking spray
- 1 scoop Blogilates Sculpt + Debloat Chocolate Shake Protein Powder
- 1 tablespoon cocoa powder
- ¼ cup liquid egg whites
- 2 tablespoons non-dairy milk
- 1 tablespoon drippy peanut butter
- 2 tablespoons granular monk fruit sweetener
- 1 tablespoon sugar-free chocolate chips
- ½ teaspoon baking powder
- Pinch sea salt

Method

1. Coat the bottom of a ramekin with cooking spray.

2. Whisk all ingredients together in a small bowl and pour into a mug or ramekin.

3. Microwave for 1:30-1:45 minutes or bake at 350 degrees for 15 minutes.*

* If you like a gooey cake, choose less cook time.

Calories: 242 | Protein: 19g | Fat: 13g | Carbs: 43g | Fiber: 6g | Net-Carbs: 8g

Lemon Mug Cake

Yield: 1 serving
Serving Size: 1 cake
Prep Time: 5 min
Cook Time: 2 min

Ingredients

- Nonstick cooking spray
- 1 scoop (23g) Blogilates Sculpt + Debloat Sweet Cream Protein Powder
- 3 tablespoons almond flour
- 1 egg
- 2 tablespoons granular monk fruit sweetener
- 2 teaspoons coconut oil, ghee or butter
- Zest of ½ medium lemon
- 2½ tablespoon lemon juice (about one medium lemon)
- ½ teaspoon baking powder
- blueberries (optional)

Method

1. Coat the bottom of a glass mug or ramekin with cooking spray.

2. Whisk all ingredients together in a small bowl and pour into prepared mug.

3. Microwave for 1:30-1:45 minutes (watching closely for overflow) or bake at 350 degrees for 15 minutes.*

4. Feel free to stir in a handful of blueberries before cooking for a colorful and delicious flavor profile.

5. Top with powdered monk fruit sweetener, if desired.
*If you like a gooey cake, choose less cook time.

Calories: 339 | Protein: 19g | Fat: 25g | Carbs: 35g | Fiber: 4g | Net-Carbs: 7g

Chocolate Protein Fudge

"Is it just me or is cutting a perfectly clean slice of chilled fudge one of the most satisfying feelings ever? Just me? Oh. Ok."

Yield: 8 serving
Serving Size: 1 fudge square
Prep Time: 5 min
Cook Time: 1 min
Freeze Time: 1 hr

Ingredients

- ¼ cup drippy nut butter or sunflower butter*
- ¼ cup melted coconut oil, browned butter or ghee*
- 2 scoops Blogilates Sculpt + Debloat Chocolate Shake Protein Powder
- 2 tablespoons powdered monk fruit Sweetener
- Pinch sea salt

Method

1. Add the nut butter to the melted oil/ghee in a medium bowl. Microwave for 30 seconds.

2. Stir until thin and smooth. Stir in the protein powder, sweetener and salt.

3. Pour into a mini loaf pan and freeze for 1 hour, or until solid.

4. Cut into 8 squares. Store in the fridge or freezer.

5. *For our favorite version, we used browned butter.

Calories: 113 | Protein: 4g | Fat: 10g | Carbs: 5g | Fiber: 1g | Net-Carbs: 1g

Chocolate Cherry Chia Parfait

"Now THIS is glamour in a cup. I mean, it's basically black tie wedding dessert table appropriate."

Yield: 2 servings
Serving Size: 1 parfait
Prep Time: 10 min
Cook Time: 5 min
Chill Time: 4 hrs

Ingredients

- 2 cups frozen cherries
- 4 tablespoons powdered monk fruit sweetener, divided
- 2 tablespoons water
- ⅔ cup non-dairy milk
- ¼ cup chia seeds
- 1 scoop Blogilates Sculpt + Debloat Chocolate Shake Protein Powder
- 1 tablespoon cocoa powder
- 1 teaspoon vanilla extract
- ⅓ cup sugar-free chocolate chips

Method

1. Add the cherries, 2 tablespoons of sweetener, and water to a small saucepan. Heat over medium and stir until the cherries are warm. Mash slightly. Pour off the cherry juice into a medium bowl. Set cherries aside to cool, then chill in the refrigerator.

2. Add the milk, chia, protein powder, remaining 2 tablespoons of sweetener, cocoa powder and vanilla to the bowl with the cherry juice. Whisk until fully combined and lump-free. Refrigerate for a minimum of 4 hours, or until thick.

3. Assemble two parfaits by alternating spoonfuls of the chia mixture, cherries, and chocolate chips.

Calories: 349 | Protein: 11g | Fat: 16g | Carbs: 77g | Fiber: 15g | Net-Carbs: 22g

No-Churn
Vanilla Protein Ice Cream

"You KNOW how much I love ice cream. I live for it. This right here is straight up sorcery."

Yield: 3 servings
Serving Size: 1 scoop
Prep Time: 5 min
Freeze Time: 4 hrs

Ingredients

- 1 (14 oz) can full-fat coconut milk
- 3 scoops (69g) Blogilates Sculpt + Debloat
    Sweet Cream Protein Powder
- 3 tablespoons granular monk fruit sweetener
- 1 teaspoon vanilla extract
- Pinch sea salt

Method

1. Add coconut milk to a blender and process for 30 seconds. Add protein powder, sweetener, vanilla, and salt and blend until thick and creamy, about 30 seconds..

2. Transfer to a medium-sized metal bowl. Lightly stir every 30 minutes for 4 hours, or until firm.

3. Cover the bowl with foil if not consuming right away, then allow to soften for 10-15 minutes before stirring and eating.

4. For a flavor variation, simply add your favorite chopped mix-ins such as strawberries, sprinkles, chocolate chips, or nuts.

Calories: 194 | Protein: 9g | Fat: 14g | Carbs: 18g | Fiber: 2g | Net-Carbs: 4g

Mixed-Berry
Protein
Nice Cream

"Perfect for a summer afternoon lounging by the pool in your fave bikini. Or honestly wherever wearing anything."

Yield: 2 servings
Serving Size: ½ recipe
Prep Time: 5 min

Ingredients

- 2½ cups frozen mixed berries (such as raspberries, cherries, and blueberries)
- 2 scoops Blogilates Sculpt + Debloat Sweet Cream Protein Powder
- 1 tablespoon powdered monk fruit sweetener
- 3-5 tablespoons non-dairy milk*

Method

1. Add all ingredients to a food processor and process until fluffy and smooth, about 3 minutes. Enjoy right away!

2. *You only want to add enough milk to ensure the food processor spins well. If you add too much, you'll get a smoothie, so allow the air to whip into the dessert by not overdoing the milk.

Calories: 141 | Protein: 9g | Fat: 0g | Carbs: 31g | Fiber: 6g | Net-Carbs: 19g

S'mores Cake Pops

Yield: 10 servings
Serving Size: 1 cake pop
Prep Time: 10 min
Cook Time: 2 min
Chill Time: 15 min

Ingredients

- 4 sheets gluten-free graham crackers, broken into pieces
- 2 scoops Blogilates Sculpt + Debloat Sweet Cream Protein Powder
- 2 tablespoons coconut flour
- 2 tablespoons granular monk fruit sweetener
- 3 tablespoons melted coconut butter
- 3 tablespoons non-dairy milk
- 1 tablespoon natural cashew butter (or nut butter of choice)
- 1 tablespoon melted coconut oil
- ½ teaspoon vanilla extract
- Pinch salt
- ⅔ cup sugar-free chocolate chips
- 1 teaspoon coconut oil

Method

1. Add the graham cracker pieces, protein powder, coconut flour, and sweetener into a food processor and process to fine crumbs.

2. Add in the coconut butter, milk, cashew butter, coconut oil, vanilla, and salt. Process until well combined and mixture sticks together when pressed.

3. Roll into 10 balls and place on parchment paper. Move to the freezer for 15 minutes. Remove from freezer and gently insert lollipop sticks.

4. Meanwhile, melt the chocolate with oil in a microwave in 30-second increments (about 2 minutes) until smooth and glossy.

5. Carefully dip and drizzle each pop with melted chocolate. Tap the stick against the edge of the bowl to remove excess chocolate.

6. Return to parchment paper and allow the chocolate to harden (about 20 minutes). Enjoy right away, or store in the refrigerator.

Calories: 148 | Protein: 4g | Fat: 10g | Carbs: 18g | Fiber: 3g | Net-Carbs: 6g

Super Fluff Ice Cream

"The best part is watching it grow. It's kinda mesmerizing."

Yield: 2 servings
Serving Size: ½ the recipe
Prep Time: 5 min
Cook Time: 2 min

Ingredients

- 1½ cups ice cubes
- 2 scoops Blogilates Sculpt + Debloat Chocolate Shake Protein Powder
- 2 frozen bananas, sliced
- ½ cup non-dairy milk
- 2 tablespoons powdered monk fruit sweetener
- 1 tablespoon powdered peanut butter such as PB2
- 1 tablespoon cocoa powder
- ½-1 teaspoon xanthan gum*

Method

1. Add ice cubes to a blender or food processor and pulse until crushed like snow.

2. Add protein powder and bananas and pulse until combined.

3. Add remaining ingredients and process until super fluffy, about 5 minutes.

*Xanthan gum is a thickener and the key ingredient to making fluff. Should you wish to omit, it will be far less airy and fluffy. Select 1 teaspoon for extra fluff.

Calories: 190 | Protein: 11g | Fat: 2g | Carbs: 47g | Fiber: 8g | Net-Carbs: 27g

Collagen Beauty Bark

Yield: 14 servings
Serving Size: 1 piece
Prep Time: 5 min
Cook Time: 2 min
Chill Time: 15 min

Ingredients

- ¾ cup sugar-free chocolate chips
- ½ cup coconut oil
- 2 scoops Blogilates Beauty Collagen Peptides
- 2 tablespoons coconut flakes
- 2 tablespoons chopped pecans
- Pinch sea salt

Method

1. Melt the chocolate and oil in a large glass measuring cup in the microwave for about 2 minutes, or until smooth, stirring every 30 seconds.

2. Stir in the collagen.

3. Line a small baking sheet with parchment paper and pour the melted chocolate on top in a thin layer. Sprinkle with coconut, pecans, and salt. Freeze for 15 minutes, then break into 14 pieces. Store in the freezer.

Calories: 122 | Protein: 2g | Fat: 12g | Carbs: 6g | Fiber: 1g | Net-Carbs: 1g

Flourless Chocolate Torte

Yield: 10 servings
Serving Size: 1 slice
Prep Time: 10 min
Cook Time: 20 min

Ingredients

- 9 oz (1½ cups) sugar-free chocolate chips (milk or semi-sweet)
- 2 teaspoons coconut oil or butter
- 2 scoops Blogilates Beauty Collagen Peptides
- 4 eggs, separated
- 1 teaspoon vanilla extract
- ¼ teaspoon salt

Method

1. Heat oven to 350°F. Line the bottom of a 6- or 7-inch springform pan with parchment paper and coat lightly and up the sides with cooking spray.

2. Microwave the chocolate and oil in a glass bowl in 30-second increments, stirring each time, until smooth (about 2 minutes). Stir in the collagen.

3. Separate the egg yolks from whites. Place the whites in a bowl of a stand mixer, or bowl in order to use a hand mixer. Whip to soft peaks.

4. Stir the yolks, vanilla, and salt into the chocolate. This will seize up the melted chocolate, but keep stirring with the back of a spoon until incorporated.

5. Fold the chocolate into the whites until fully combined. If needed, use your mixer on low to incorporate.

6. Pour into the pan and bake for 18-20 minutes, leaving the center slightly underdone. It will fully set when cooled.

Calories: 148 | Protein: 6g | Fat: 11g | Carbs: 16g | Fiber: 3g | Net-Carbs: 2g

Berry Crumble Bars

Yield: 16 servings
Serving Size: 1 bar
Prep Time: 10 min
Cook Time: 23 min

Ingredients

Crumble:
- 1 cup oat flour
- 1 cup old fashioned oats
- 2 scoops Blogilates Sculpt + Debloat Sweet Cream Protein Powder
- ½ cup granular monk fruit sweetener
- ¼ teaspoon baking soda
- ¼ teaspoon salt
- 10 tablespoons melted butter or coconut oil
- 1 teaspoon vanilla extract
- 1 tablespoon water*

Filling:
- 2½ cups (12 oz bag) frozen blueberries, cherries or mixed berries
- ¼ cup granular monk fruit sweetener
- 1 tablespoon arrowroot powder or tapioca flour

Method

1. Heat oven to 350°F. Line the bottom of a 9-by-9-inch baking dish with parchment paper.

2. Whisk together the oat flour, oats, protein powder, sweetener, baking soda, and salt. Stir in the butter/oil and vanilla extract. *Add water if the crumble needs a bit more moisture. It should be able to stick together when pressed between two fingers.

3. Firmly press ¾ of the crumble into the bottom of the pan and set aside.

4. Make the filling by adding the frozen berries to a small pot with the sweetener and stir over medium heat for 5 minutes or until syrupy. Stir in the arrowroot/tapioca until the mixture thickens a bit, then pour over the crumble base.

5. Sprinkle the reserved crumble over the top and bake for 23-25 minutes or until the top crumble is golden.

Calories: 118 | Protein: 3g | Fat: 8g | Carbs: 15g | Fiber: 2g | Net-Carbs: 7g

Published in the United States by oGorgeous Inc.
Blogilates © | blogilates.com
16350 Ventura Blvd
Suite D #334
Encino, CA 91436

Recipes developed by Erin Woodbury
and Cassey Ho
Recipes tested by Erin Woodbury and
Breanna Woods, R.D.
Macronutrients by Breanna Woods, R.D.
Cover photography by Sam Livits
Food photography by Kateryna Parshukova
Food styling by Kateryna Parshukova
Lifestyle photography by Sam Livits
Cover Design and art direction by
Brittney Brandt
Book design by Kirsten Haakonsen
Title: Sculpt. A protein cookbook.
Recipes to feed the joy in fitness /
by Cassey Ho
ISBN: 978-0-578-38125-1
First edition
Printed in China